CAT
ZODIAC

AN ASTROLOGICAL GUIDE
TO THE FELINE MYSTIQUE

MAEVA CONSIDINE ILLUSTRATIONS BY **VIKKI CHU**

CHRONICLE BOOKS
SAN FRANCISCO

Library of Congress Cataloging-in-Publication Data

Considine, Maeva.

  Cat zodiac : an astrological guide to the feline mystique / by Maeva Considine ; illustrations by Vikki Chu.

    pages cm

  ISBN 978-1-4521-4828-1

  1. Astrology and pets. 2. Horoscopes. 3. Cats--Miscellanea. I. Title.

  BF1728.3.C66 2016

  133.5'86368--dc23

          2015024026

Manufactured in China

MIX
Paper from
responsible sources
FSC
www.fsc.org
FSC™ C104723

Written by Maeva Considine

Illustrated by Vikki Chu

Designed by Hillary Caudle

10 9 8 7 6 5 4 3 2 1

Chronicle Books LLC
680 Second Street
San Francisco, California 94107
www.chroniclebooks.com

CONTENTS

INTRODUCTION

"In ancient times cats were worshipped
as gods; they have not forgotten this."
TERRY PRATCHETT

If you've picked up this book, chances are you own a cat or are close with someone who owns a cat; or maybe you've been thinking about getting a cat and you want to know—for better or worse—exactly what you're getting yourself into.

The good news is that you are not alone in your curiosity about the desires and intentions of our furry feline friends. A comprehensive understanding of cats has eluded us for the nearly 5,300 years of the domestication of the species. *Cat Zodiac* will show you how to interpret your cat's actions, relationships, and desires based on his or her zodiac sign. If you don't know when your feline companion was born, this book will also help you determine what sign your cat was likely born under, with the help of a personality chart found after this section, which highlights the strongest traits of each sign.

Whether you're a brand-new cat owner, have lived with a feline companion or two for years, or are just intrigued by the feline mystique, this book is here to aid you in demystifying cat personalities, using the stars as your guide.

While there has been some successful research into the physiology of cats, much of what we know about the emotions of our friends in fur has been left to assumption and speculation. What we do know is that the domesticated cat has a long and regal history of companionship with humans, dating back to the time of ancient Egypt. We also know that cats have been the focus of many cultures' mythos, and that much of their charm is owed to the seductive elusiveness not found in other domesticated animals.

The closest relatives to the domesticated cat are believed to have first appeared in China, drawn to villages from their mountain dwellings for the abundance of rodents. These cats ended up moving much closer, and eventually into, human dwellings where access to food and warmth was easily attained. Once the cats were domesticated, it was clear to many ancient cultures that these animals possessed a great deal of intelligence and personality that set them apart from the other domesticated species of the times. So great was this distinction that some societies began worshipping them as deities. In Egypt, the goddess of fire and cats, Bastet, was often depicted with the body of a woman and the head of a lioness. Her form was later represented with the head of a black cat after Egyptians began to bring felines into their homes as pets. Cats in Egypt were sacred, revered as guides to the souls of their human counterparts. Cats were often mummified and buried with pharaohs to guide them on their journey to the afterlife. The domesticated cat has played many roles in mythology, some stranger than others. In Norse history, goddess of love Freyja is often shown with a chariot drawn by strong, sleek cats.

Today, cats are still exalted in Japan, where statues of the calico Japanese Bobtail, known as *maneki-neko* ("lucky cat"), are placed outside storefronts and homes to bring good luck and financial prosperity to families; and the phenomenon of Japanese cat cafés has taken root in the United States, where the cafés are starting to find footing. Online, cats from all around the world are the subjects of millions of viral videos; and several celebrity felines have gained enough notoriety from these videos that they tour the country to promote their appearances in books, movies, and commercials.

The mysterious nature of the cat has not always been viewed in a positive light. In many cultures, cats are thought to bring bad luck, particularly black cats, which were once believed to belong to powerful covens of witches, acting as familiars to carry out a witch's bidding. To this day, it is still considered bad luck in many places if a black cat crosses your path. Fortunately, much of this negative speculation about cats has turned into a dull hum

of superstition well below the roar of supporters—those who believe that cats wield their mysterious powers for good, to help guide humans through the confusion and frustration of everyday living.

It is perhaps this long, full history of companionship that fuels our desire to figure out just what our cat wants when she talks to us or pushes a full glass of water from the table to the floor.

Fortunately, where modern science has failed to explain the actions of these creatures, astrology has come to uncover some of the more cryptic facets of cat ownership.

For nearly two thousand years, people have turned to astrological charts for answers and guidance to life's more difficult queries. Typically, we have used these charts and signs to interpret our own behavior, but as cats become more integrated into our lives, the zodiac can be an extremely useful tool to determine the motivations of our furry friends. *Cat Zodiac* will tell you how to use these twelve Sun signs to better interpret feline behavior, traits, and personalities. Zodiac is a Greek word that describes the circular division of twelve longitudes of the sun's path. In astronomy this divides the night sky we see into twelve parts, and in astrology it divides the year into twelve parts, giving us the twelve sun signs described in this book.

Babylon is credited with creating the science of astrology over three millennia ago, when they came up with ways to chart the stars to better predict and understand the seasons of the Earth. They shared these findings with the Greeks and then the Romans, who would use this knowledge to predict cosmic events, agricultural development, weather forecasts, wars, natural disasters, and famine. At the time, these scholars believed that there were five planets: Mercury, Mars, Saturn, Jupiter, and Venus, and that each planet possessed unique powers over the known universe with the ability to temper or engage certain emotions in Earth's inhabitants. Much of this philosophy about the planets remains deeply engrained in zodiac culture. As you will read in this book, each sun sign has a ruling planet that holds strong influence over those born under its correlating sign.

The Egyptians also had a deep appreciation of the zodiac, and perhaps the earliest recordation of the classic twelve sun signs are found in the Dendera zodiac, a piece of ceiling from the Hathor temple built during the Ptolemaic period (305 BC–30 BC). These early people knew that the Earth and the sun were intrinsically connected, and that the appearance of a certain constellation meant a change in seasons, bringing along with it a sway in the attitudes and personalities of those born during these times. Today Western society focuses on the sun signs' relationships to the seasons rather than their relationships to the constellations we see in the night sky. For this reason, you may find that different publications, books, and experts list different start and end dates to each sun sign. The ruling houses break down the zodiac calendar even further by creating a second wheel that measures a twenty-four hour cycle on Earth. This means that you could have two very different Leo kitties because they were born under different ruling houses. For simplicity, *Cat Zodiac* will use one ruling house as an example for each sun sign.

The zodiac of the West also focuses on the polarities of the signs (masculine and feminine) and the qualities of each sign (Cardinal signs, Fixed signs, and Mutable signs). The polarities divide the twelve signs into two groups of six. The six feminine signs are believed to be more passive while the six masculine signs are thought to be more assertive at their core. The qualities of the zodiac, also known as the modes of the zodiac or the Quadruplicities, divide the twelve signs into three groups with four sun signs assigned to each group. The Cardinal signs are inventive and centered on the self. The Fixed signs are happy with routine and schedule and don't often change their minds. The Mutable signs are ever changing and evolving and because of this they tend to go with the flow.

The twelve constellations are also divided into four categories: fire signs, water signs, Earth signs, and air signs. These categories can be used to further dissect and interpret the behavior of each sun sign. For instance, if your cat seems most cordial in the summer time she is likely using the power of the fire sign Leo to attract extra attention from you.

The zodiac's timeless popularity and uncanny ability to decode the essence of those born underneath the twelve constellations has sealed its fate as an integral predictor of animal behavior. We hope that this book will bring you to a closer understanding of your feline companion. You will find in these pages information on each of the zodiac signs and what to expect in your cat's personality, lifestyle, and relationships, bringing you closer to understanding how best to cater to your cat's needs.

Are you unsure of when your feline companion was born? If you started your journey with your cat without an official birth date in hand, consult the chart on the following pages which outlines the more dominant personalities and behaviors typical to each sign. This chart is also handy if you're considering bringing a new cat into your home, and are curious of the primary personality markers of each sun sign.

The power of myth and mysterious aura will always surround our cat friends—that is part of the wonder and the spectacle of their presence—but with understanding comes deeper connections and happiness for both you and your cat. Your friend will surely appreciate your efforts to get to know her better . . . even if she still insists on sleeping in the fresh laundry.

PERSONALITIES OF THE ZODIAC

♈
ARIES
THE BUSINESSMAN

Bold
Freethinker
Juvenile
Social

♉
TAURUS
THE ACTIVIST

Self-important
Friendly
Tastemaker
Begrudging

♊
GEMINI
THE TWO SOULS

Charming
Emotionally Stunted
Creative
Loving

♋
CANCER
THE COLLECTOR

Tenderhearted
Highly Social
Easily Wounded
Sentimental

♌
LEO
THE LAWYER

Deep Thinker
Tempestuous
Driven
Stoic

♍
VIRGO
THE DOER

Natural Leader
Pragmatic
Insipid
Regimented

♎ LIBRA
THE JUDGE

Orderly

Punctual

Philanthropic

Law-loving

♏ SCORPIO
THE HUNTER

Timeless

Sharp

Undaunted

Ruthless Provider

♐ SAGITTARIUS
THE ATHLETE

Sharp-witted

High Energy

Warmhearted

Eager

♑ CAPRICORN
THE CLIMBER

Old Soul

Charming

Cunning

Traitorous

♒ AQUARIUS
THE PHILOSOPHER

Pondering

Slow-moving

Defensive

Tactical

♓ PISCES
THE SWIMMER

Sweet

Slow

Easily Swayed

Laid-back

ARIES

MARCH 21 TO APRIL 20

BOLD, SURPRISING, COMFORTING, IDEALISTIC

SYMBOL	The Ram
ELEMENT	Fire
QUALITY	Cardinal
RULING HOUSE	First
RULING PLANET	Mars
POLARITY	Masculine
LUCKY STONE	Diamonds
LUCKY NUMBER	9

PERSONALITY

The Aries has the distinction of being the first sign of the zodiac, and you will find that your cat embodies this distinction in his own life. He is probably first to the food bowl in the morning, first to tell you when it's time to be let outside, and first to tell you when his needs aren't being met. This boldness is actually a wonderful quality for your ram to have, as cats can generally be elusive, but it is rare for the Aries to go long without making it clear what he wants.

These cats love surprises and changing environments. Your Ram probably finds the outdoors—or the essence of the outdoors—thrilling, so he will be at your feet the minute you come in the door, sniffing and talking to you about what he's experiencing. These are talkative cats with

a predilection for hilarious and well-timed vocalizations. Aries doesn't like to be left without some company, so these cats often enjoy the company of other felines. You will see your Aries quickly assert himself as the alpha of the group. You may find your Aries trying to join you in the bathroom when you're showering, just to chat about his day or to tell you when he needs a treat or two. Your cat wears his heart on his paw, so you'll notice he may bounce between vocal and quiet when he is upset or hurt.

The Aries lives life to the fullest and will often perform daring stunts to keep his high-octane brain entertained. This adventurous nature will have you discovering your Ram asleep in strange places like the top of the refrigerator or the top shelf of the linen closet. These cats require lots of love and attention, but the humor and joy they return is worth the effort, tenfold.

LIFESTYLE

If you've owned your Ram cat for even a short amount of time, you know these cats don't settle. They are highly competitive and will compete for the other people and animals in your life to gain your undivided attention. It is recommended that the average indoor cat should get at least fifteen minutes of intentional play a day, but you may find that your Aries requires even more than that, plus lots of extra time for cuddling. It can be difficult for Aries to learn they are not the center of the universe, so don't be afraid to say no to these cats once in a while, as it will help them grow emotionally.

Aries felines are some of the cuddliest cats in the zodiac, so leaving out a nice lavender-infused blanket will help calm their zesty attitudes and bring them the comfort they desire. Your Aries is ruled by the head, and his desire for big things in life can lead him to want big meals. Counteract this by feeding your cat a balanced diet and laying off the treats, even when he begs. Because these cats also require a lot of stimulation, adaptive or movable toys suit their personality best. Light-up balls, crinkle toys, and mice will entertain your Ram for hours, but be sure to mix up the collection and stow away favorite toys from time to time to keep things fresh.

The Aries is a light sleeper who prefers to squeeze every second out of life and is a bit more nocturnal than the other cats of the zodiac. Storing away toys and playthings when not in use and propping your bedroom door open for when he tuckers out and needs a comfy bed to nap on are two good ways to keep your friend happy in the evening and nighttime hours. Because the Ram is a fire sign, your cat will likely do best in cool, dry environments; so, if you can't find your kitty right away, be sure to search the cupboards and the bathtub; wherever he is, you'll probably find him content in his element.

RELATIONSHIPS

Leo, Sagittarius, Gemini

Aries are passionate creatures and are prone to showing affection in spurts and phases. This can mean you spend your days with two different kinds of cat in one cat body: quiet and reserved, then passionate and fun. Leo, like Aries, loves being at the center of things, and these two can learn to achieve a harmony sharing the spotlight. The Gemini loves a challenge and will drive the Aries in his competitive nature to new experiences and new heights. With the Sagittarius, the Aries will find warmth and mutual respect and thirst for knowledge.

Your Aries is a passionate cat who will enjoy watching you go about your day. He will make you pause and appreciate the goodness of having someone in your life that loves you and waits for you to get home at the end of the day. Don't take it personally when your Ram needs his space. His life is in nearly constant motion and sometimes he can overwhelm himself. He will probably want to remain near you during these times, but will also want space to collect his bearings. Be mindful of his temperaments and don't to ignore the Aries' feelings or desires for too long—even though these are tough cats on the outside, their emotions can be very raw and fiery.

This cat will love long strokes across his back and scratches at the base of his tail, though he may not like to be held or cradled. But don't be mistaken: these are cats that love laps and rolling around to get your attention. The Ram travels well, so if you are looking for a road companion or simply a cat who handles moves well, this is the type of cat you are looking for. Some may say that dog is man's best friend, but those people likely have never had the pleasure of meeting an adventurous Aries cat.

TAURUS
APRIL 21 to MAY 21

STOIC, DEVOTED, OBSTINATE, DECISIVE

SYMBOL	The Bull
ELEMENT	Earth
QUALITY	Fixed
RULING HOUSE	Second
RULING PLANET	Venus
POLARITY	Feminine
LUCKY STONE	Sapphire
LUCKY NUMBER	15

PERSONALITY

The Taurus feline is a bold, Earth-centered animal who thirsts for the finer things life has to offer. Cats born under this star will shine at house parties with their vocal tendencies and frequent demands for physical affection. The Taurus is a commanding, feminine presence and delights at her position in center stage.

Taurus cats love bringing people together, and seem to have boundless energy when there is a crowd of adoring fans around; though when the house is quiet, the Taurus prefers to sleep the day away in comfort and harmony. When she's awake, the Taurus always has a plan, and there is little that can be done to change her direction. As kittens, Taureans are very talkative and gregarious creatures, and typically keep that boisterous personality for life. The

Taurus cat becomes more dependent on routine as she ages, thus most Taureans thrive in an environment with consistency and dependability.

The Taurus loves her personal space and she is very good at retreating quietly when she needs to find her inner peace. And while your Taurean will always be willing to remind you when it is time to be fed or the litter box is in need of attention, she expects these things to be taken care of before she has to ask. While the Taurus is not fond of surprises, she can be coaxed into trying new and fine things. A fresh catnip-dipped mouse or a shiny new ball will be welcome tokens of your affection. As a bold and big personality, the Taurus may have trouble sharing the limelight with you or other pets. Because of this she often works better alone, but she will make meaningful connections with the right companions. The Taurus is not a low-maintenance cat, but with the right amount of pampering and attention, she will become your most loyal and devoted friend, bringing Earth-centered balance to your home.

LIFESTYLE

The Taurus cat doesn't settle for the store-bought cat bed or generic label cat food; and, quite frankly, why should this beautiful, intelligent animal have to? She prefers to lie in the comfort of a cashmere sweater left unattended on the bed and to eat only the finest selections off of her human's dinner plate.

The Taurus is a comfortingly dependable creature. You will often find that she eats, naps, and takes strolls around the same time every day, but this constant need to maintain stasis will also make her uncomfortable in the face of change. She is adaptable, but try your best to be mindful of her treasured routine. If your Taurus is struggling with her emotions, she will make it clear. It is best to let her work things out in her own time, either by letting her out into the garden for a balancing solo stroll or opening up a warm hamper full of fresh laundry to lounge in.

The Taurus can be a very opinionated feline, so you will want to try a variety of treats and meals before she finds the things that please her refined palate, and she won't settle for anything less than perfection. The Taurean also enjoys naps like most felines, but prefers to wake frequently throughout the day for long, meandering stretches and luxurious baths in the midafternoon sun. It's best to place several scratching posts in different rooms around your home for the Taurus cat. Since she takes great pleasure in maintaining her beautiful nails, she will reward you with untouched furniture. The Taurean also prefers several high perches for those times when her emotions get the best of her (especially if she is an indoor cat). A tall cat tree will give your Taurus that commanding feeling she craves and her personality will flourish with a space of her own. Don't forget to treat the Taurus frequently to delicious, healthy snacks or a new toy. She will use these as props to gain a crowd's full attention, performing tricks and responding to commands that other cats would find difficult to comprehend.

RELATIONSHIPS

BEST MATCHES	Scorpio, Virgo, Capricorn

The Taurean likes companionship, which allows her to maintain her treasured equilibrium, but she has no problem going it alone. For this reason the observant Scorpio would make the perfect human mate who is capable of timing these moods and adjusting quickly to the Taurean's ever-changing needs. The independent Virgo will not only give the Taurus the space she desires, she will also give the Bull her beloved limelight. The Virgo has little desire for fame or being fawned over and will enjoy watching the Taurus shine bright in her element. The detail-oriented Capricorn won't let the whimsical and easily distracted Taurus stray too far from the fold.

She will help her hone her focus and provide her with the firmness the bull desperately needs.

The Taurus is a lap cat when she wants to be, and a lone wolf when she needs to be. Do not take offense if your Taurus doesn't run to greet you at the door—she will come to you when it feels right, making your interactions with one another more authentic. The Taurus prefers bold affection and may display some lovingly dominant behaviors like head-butting. The reserved Scorpios, Virgos, and Capricorns will be buoyed up by this positive and boisterous energy on particularly draining days. The Taurus is known for her ability to help diminish or dismiss emotional insecurities in others. She is fiercely and determinately loyal, which builds confidence in these apprehensive sun signs.

With companion animals, the Taurus behaves much the same as with humans. She would prefer to have her own sunny spot on the couch, but with the right mate the Taurus will have no problem cuddling up to her feline friend for comfort and security. If you let her, the Taurus will be the life of every party.

GEMINI

MAY 22 TO JUNE 21

HUMOROUS, EASYGOING, VERSATILE, STRONG

SYMBOL	The Twins
ELEMENT	Air
QUALITY	Cardinal
RULING HOUSE	Third
RULING PLANET	Mercury
POLARITY	Masculine
LUCKY STONE	Topaz
LUCKY NUMBER	14

PERSONALITY

Ying and Yang, the Twins sign of the zodiac, have perfected the art of being Zen, flexible, goofy, and hilarious all at the same time. These are the cats that have their own YouTube channels and large fan followings. The third ruling house never shies away from trying something new, even if it means taking it on the chin from time to time. These cats like to test boundaries and are known to disappear from time to time to adventure into new places. When they return from these mysterious getaways, they tend to seem wiser and calmer. Though these excursions may make your Gemini seem like an unruly teenager, he's not out partying—he is simply looking for outlets for his abundance of energy and brain power.

Your Gemini has a masculine polarity and does not like to be stifled, so it may be hard to keep this guy indoors for too long. He may find the call of the outside landscape too strong to resist and will try his best to escape confined, small spaces. Let him go out and explore, even if it's just within the confines of your apartment and you'll be rewarded with respect and dedication when your Gemini comes back to you.

The Gemini loves to make others laugh, even at his own expense. Mistimed jumps, sleeping on his back with his legs up in the air, and stealing entire plates of human food are not unknown stunts to the Gemini. These are cats with big, big personalities who see time as something best spent doing the things they love, even if it means leaving the world of comfort for a while. When a Gemini is in the right mood, he will shower you with love and affection and tell you all about his adventures and the sights he has seen. All he is looking for in the world is a sympathetic ear to listen to his stories and a very large domain to explore.

LIFESTYLE

As you've probably already discovered if you own a Twins cat, the Gemini cat does not take containment well. These are the escape artists of the zodiac, so if you insist on having an indoor Gemini, be sure to include lots and lots of walks on a leash through the neighborhood. These are born entertainers, so providing them with a lot of verbal encouragement will bring out the ham in your kitty. These cats are also known to go out and disappear from time to time. If your Gemini is an outdoor kitty, don't panic if you don't see him right away when you get home from work; he's probably over at the neighbors' house entertaining them or stealing their cat's food.

These cats don't require a lot of upkeep. If your Gemini wants something he'll usually go out and get it himself:

toys, attention, and scratches on the back. But be sure to feed your Gemini a diet that will support his joints, since they will get a lot of use in his lifetime. The Gemini cat also loves high spaces. Don't be surprised or concerned to see your cat up a tree or on the roof of your garage; they are expert climbers, constantly testing the limits of their own bodies. Your cat's physique will benefit from this active inclination and from lots of indoor play if he can't go outside. A "mouse on a string," feather teaser, and other toys that keep up the speed will be a sound investment for your friend. He will also appreciate you joining him at his level during playtime; don't be afraid to get down and let your Gemini show you his wild side.

RELATIONSHIPS

BEST MATCHES   Aquarius, Libra, Aries

There are few cats in the world like the Gemini cat: his thirst for adventure and need to stimulate his brain can make him hard company to keep up with, but if the Gemini finds his soulmate, it may ignite that spark that will give this amazing feline the energy and fun he needs to live a long and healthy life.

The right human will know when to bring the Gemini back down to Earth for some much needed rest, which is where the level-headed Libra would do well with a Gemini companion. Neither of these signs is prone to jealousy, so the human Libra can go about her business without hurting the Gemini's feelings. Geminis don't often feel rebuffed;

instead, they turn that pent-up energy to zooming around the living room, or climbing up the cat tree and back down again several times, leaving his Libra human to do her work in almost-peace. Much like the Gemini, the Aquarius is full of surprises, and this pairing will bring explosive fun to any home environment. The Aquarius also has a broad mind and will come up with fun challenges for the Gemini, keeping him stimulated.

The best match for the Gemini will know that these cats are capable of a lot, and require a lot of stimulation and rest time to keep them functioning at optimal levels. This relationship will require work and balance, but with the right companion the Gemini cat will learn when it is time to put on a show and when it is time to pump the brakes and just enjoy being in the same room together. The Gemini is a great writing partner, reading partner, and art partner. Let him guide you when you've hit a creative wall. Ten minutes playing with this cat and you will feel inspired to do big things in your own life. The worst thing you can do for yourself and your Gemini is to leave his potential untapped. Make the most of every day with these cats and you will feel more creative, appreciated, and energetic than you ever have before. There is a kinetic energy present in these creatures that has the ability to inspire affection and forgiveness for these two-sided creatures.

CANCER

JUNE 22 TO JULY 23

DIPLOMATIC, ROOTED, AUTOCRATIC, CHARMING

SYMBOL	The Crab
ELEMENT	Water
QUALITY	Cardinal
RULING HOUSE	Fourth
RULING PLANET	Moon
POLARITY	Feminine
LUCKY STONE	Emerald
LUCKY NUMBER	11

PERSONALITY

The Crab is tough and has weathered a lot of storms. Your Crab kitty may have showed up on your doorstep one day like an old, leathery sailor, or maybe you picked her up from a shelter because she had been there the longest and had outlasted the cuteness of kitten season. Either way, these cats are rough-and-tumble on the outside, but deep down they are fastidious cats with incredible memories.

Your Cancer will adapt to your routine in no time. She will learn to read your moods quickly, and is always looking for a way to bring a diplomatic peace to the home. The Cancer will often sacrifice her own feelings if it will bring harmony to the group. These are traditionalist cats who prefer to stay close to home. They are ruled by the moon, which means they are prone to the occasional moodiness that comes with the change of the lunar cycle; but this also means they get a chance to reset and will likely keep this moodiness from affecting the energy of the home.

Though not always a cuddly creature, the Cancer cat is loyal to the bitter end. By bringing a Cancer into the home, you have already given her the best gift she could ever want: shelter. This shelter is so important that Cancers can become very territorial, and have been known to wait at the door for unexpected guests, just to make sure you and the home are safe. Warn guests that you have hired a watch cat and make sure that they give these kitties plenty of praise when meeting them for the first time. This is a foolproof way to make sure your guard cat lets the right folks in. The Crab finds her own way to show affection, and it is usually through this dedication to creating a stable and safe environment. If she senses emotional instability, she will do anything she can to rectify the situation, even if it means breaking out of her normally reserved shell to make others laugh or smile. The Cancer is a sweet and tough-all-around cat who can find her way in life independently, but she does prefer to help others—especially at the time of a new moon when the world is dark and others need help finding their way.

LIFESTYLE

The stoicism of the Cancer cannot be matched. This is perhaps the lowest-maintenance cat in all of the signs in the zodiac. Your Crab would be happy with an old towel and a cardboard box. But just because she doesn't seek luxury, that doesn't mean you can't show her affection—and you should, because deep down these creatures are soft and loving. If she's willing to crawl into your lap, reward her closeness with small scraps of chicken or treats.

She may not always display her hurt or need, so be sure to look for subtle changes in behavior that will indicate what is wrong. It is rare that the Cancer would like to venture too far from the home. She usually prefers the couch or somewhere centrally located where she can guard the home and watch over her people. If she claims

a particular cushion on the couch, she will let you know, in no uncertain terms, that she is the guardian and the keeper of that cushion. Having an older chair near a door will give her the perfect perch to relax on and to use as a command post.

The Cancer cat will sometimes eat out of emotional insecurity, so it's best not to leave food lying around unnecessarily. Keep her diet balanced and portioned to avoid overeating. The Crab will also require a fitness regimen to keep her joints fit and functional, since it may be hard to get these cats to let loose and be silly. Try noisy toys in a separate room to draw her away from her comfort zone. Bring out the hunter in your Cancer, and she will likely be happy to engage in some play. Don't worry too much about schedules or houseguests with these cats; once introduced, they can grow to accept most anything you throw at them.

RELATIONSHIPS

BEST MATCHES   Taurus, Scorpio, Virgo

Like the Taurus, the Cancer feels a deep need for security and emotional balance. These two signs are very compatible and will often support each other through rough times. If you are a Taurus living alone, a Crab cat would be an excellent addition to your house. Neither of these signs tends to show outward emotion, but the undercurrent of support between these two signs will be deeply welcomed and encouraged. Scorpios crave attention and to be desired, which are two things that the Cancer is great at delivering, through her need to provide security and undivided attention. The Scorpio's passion can drive the Cancer out of her shell a bit more. It's hard not to feel inspired around a Scorpio's passionate nature. The Virgo also cares about the family and her people, and will find this common bond with the Cancer comforting. Both are also very rational creatures and not prone to argumentation, which makes for a very calm, practical home life.

If you enjoy a cat who runs by her own set of rules, but also enjoys being part of the family setting, the Cancer is your new best pal. The Cancer is maternal and will need to provide you with some measure of comfort, even if she shows it in unusual or indirect ways. Make sure you allow her to perform this function in your life, even if you're not the type to need this sort of comfort. Allowing her to do this will make both of you happy and it will help your Crab cat grow emotionally. It's not always easy to tell what's going on inside the head of a Cancer cat, but the search for answers will open you up in ways you never knew possible. These cats are capable of long-lasting, wonderful bonds with their humans that mature over the many years they can spend together.

LEO

JULY 24 TO AUGUST 23

ENTHUSIASTIC, OUTGOING, SELF-ASSURED,
AMBITIOUS

SYMBOL	**The Lion**
ELEMENT	**Fire**
QUALITY	**Fixed**
RULING HOUSE	**Fifth**
RULING PLANET	**Sun**
POLARITY	**Feminine**
LUCKY STONE	**Moonstone**
LUCKY NUMBER	**22**

PERSONALITY

Leo, the lion, is the essence of cat. Bold and majestic, these cats embody all of the celestial goodness of the lion zodiac. Your Leo will know exactly what it takes to please her, and she will stop at nothing to be center stage. Ruled by the Sun, she is regal and debonair. There is something undeniably special about the Leo cat. This is the cat who commands a room when she enters and who will have you in rapt attention for hours as she parades around the house, vocalizing everything she sees and thinks.

The Leo does not wait for attention to come to her; she is hardworking and pays close mind to her physique and her actions in order to grab the attention of those around her. She likes the finer things, but knows that with the pursuit of material goods comes dedication and work. She plays

hard and studies hard, watching the world around her and soaking in all of the beauty and joy that nature provides. She is a jovial cat who relishes making others happy, and may be disappointed when you aren't aware of her efforts.

Being ruled by the solar sign, Leo requires lots of warmth and light to keep her upbeat tempo. She will find her spot in a bay window or under a reading lamp and stay there for as long as you let her. Fixed signs are the great stabilizers of the zodiac; as such, the Leo is definitely a traditionalist and will spend a great deal of her time napping and eating. Don't let this fool you: She will get down to business when necessary. She is a natural-born star, and your family and friends will love cat sitting this gregarious and kind friend.

LIFESTYLE

Living with a Leo cat comes with both joy and responsibility. These cats are foodies who crave a high-carbohydrate diet and may try to join you during your human meals. Be sure to feed her a diet that fits her large lifestyle, but also supports her overall health, which is most important to the Leo. While she is magnanimous in her behavior, the Leo typically is very sensitive on the inside; good digestion is important for this active cat. Make sure she has plenty of clear, clean water to keep her skin and coat hydrated and her heart strong, as these are some of the most important features to her.

If you live in a cold climate, you will want to make sure she has access to a heater or a heated bed. Her temper will cool during the winter months and it will be at its warmest

during the summer months. The Leo will love to share your bed, and your warmth, so don't be surprised to find her perched on your pillow most mornings. She will have no problem sharing the bed with other cats and people, so long as she has the lion's share. The Leo is a playful cat, but she may not require the high-energy playtime that other cats desperately need.

She prefers gentle strokes and scratches, and is the perfect cat to snuggle up with on the couch to watch a movie in the dead of winter. But, watch out, come summer she will be ready to show off her well-rested physique—to your eye, this change may be like night and day. Where most cats are likely to be active in the night hours, the Leo is apt to be most alert during the daylight hours, strutting through the house surveying her territory, and she will calm once the sun has set. She is predictable and appreciates it when those around her are as well, but for new food or special treats she can make exceptions, as she's not entirely averse to adding some spice to her comfortable routine.

RELATIONSHIPS

BEST MATCHES   Sagittarius, Libra, Aries

The Leo loves to be at the head of the table, so anyone invested in a companionship with a Leo has to be prepared to give up the spotlight now and again for this outgoing creature. She will do best in a house with multiple human companions to dote on her, and perhaps a feline companion who is compatible with her personality, although the Leo can learn to adjust to a variety of situations and people.

It may be surprising that the Leo does quite well with other Leos, as they both love to be the greatest presence in the room, but it is only other Leos who can truly appreciate the love of the spotlight and the desire for finer things life has to offer. This pairing will bring a beautiful relationship of understanding and meaning to you and your cat. The Leo also connects deeply with the smart and reasonable Sagittarius, who will let Leo take the reins but who also knows how to reach her on a deeper level. In the Aries, your Leo will find another go-getter who doesn't fear self-promotion and will help Leo gain access to the things she desires. Your Leo cat will prefer to keep things lighthearted and will cherish a human companion who wants to keep her happy spirits alive for many years. The Leo appreciates other zodiac leaders, but doesn't possess their levelheadedness. That is why the Leo will thrive with someone who can keep her in line when she gets drawn too far into herself, but will do so in a way that doesn't insult her sensibilities.

By providing her with balance and attention, your Leo will be your closest friend and your truest confidant, though you may need to do some work up front to gain her trust. You must prove that you are the attentive presence she desires. Never turn down an opportunity to pet or praise your Leo so you can build the best relationship possible. When you are at home, spend time grooming her coat and pay close attention to that intrinsic quality that only she can possess. Let her solar energy bring harmony and joy to your dwelling.

VIRGO

AUGUST 24 TO SEPTEMBER 23

FASTIDIOUS, ASTUTE, CARING, STOIC

SYMBOL	The Virgin
ELEMENT	Earth
QUALITY	Mutable
RULING HOUSE	Sixth
RULING PLANET	Mercury
POLARITY	Feminine
LUCKY STONE	Jasper
LUCKY NUMBER	23

PERSONALITY

The most easygoing sign, Virgo is a mutable sign in every sense—mutable signs are the free-flowing energies in the zodiac—which can mean it's sometimes hard to even know when your Virgo is in the room. She's quiet, but it comes from a place of observing and stoicism. The motto of the Virgo is "I serve," and she is always waiting for an opportunity to be useful to those around her.

Nothing feels quite like the presence of a Virgo cat: Soothing, understanding, and sensible, she is like a warm cup of chamomile tea after a hard day of work. She may not be the social climber of the zodiac world, but that is because the earthy Virgo is grounded in her sense of self. She doesn't mind a changing routine because she knows her relationships are more important than the scenery or any fancy cat toys. She is meticulously clean, even more so than the average cat, preferring long and luxurious baths over extended playtime or roughhousing. You may be pleasantly surprised to find that she can keep the litter inside her box and the food inside her bowl. If she meows at you it's probably because she has some litter stuck between her paws and needs your help removing it.

Her meticulous nature, however, doesn't interfere with her mellow attitude. If she can't immediately find a solution to a problem, she will keep at it patiently until she gets her answer. This problem-solving trait makes the burden of caring for a Virgo cat very light. These are sweet, sweet cats who operate well in a house with busy people. She will often take a while to warm up to new friends because she prefers to observe and study others rather than interact with them. The Virgin zodiac maintains her youthful innocence and can maintain her kitten-like playfulness for many years.

LIFESTYLE

Virgo cats are full of surprises but are not excitable or overly energetic. Lounging, cleaning, and small walks are at the top of the Virgo's to-do list. She prefers the indoors, as the house is more predictable than the outside world. She'll try on different sleeping places throughout her years, but she may be more comfortable sleeping at the foot of the bed or on a pile of discarded clothes than at your head or by your side.

Virgo likes the morning hours and as the Earth comes to life, so she will likely greet the day with big stretches and sighs. Kneading blankets and clothing will comfort her greatly, and Virgos are also quite the yogis, so you may find her sitting in funny or unusual positions for a cat. These cats crave a balance between warmth and cold, and may prefer wet food over dry to fulfill this preference. Virgos tend to have a sweet tooth, so watch carefully over your desserts so your feline doesn't outsmart you and give herself a stomach upset.

These cats have sensitive nervous systems that maintain a very key emotional balance; several light meals throughout the day may suit her better than two big meals. Frequent brushings will also be important to keep up your Virgo's self-image and general cleanliness, and despite her potential protests, baths or cat-friendly wipes will also give her the cleanliness she desires. Be aware, this meticulousness toward health also extends to those around her, so you may be the unwitting subject of rough tongue baths or a set of sharp claws brushing through your hair. It can border on obsession, so try to draw your Virgo out of her own head; try filling your home with calming scents like Roman chamomile or rose to keep the Virgo from focusing too much on her physicality, giving her space to relax and enjoy the ordered world she lives in.

RELATIONSHIPS

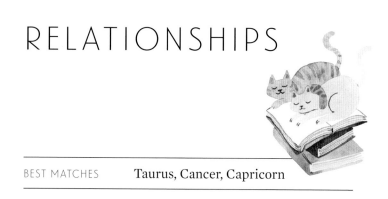

BEST MATCHES	Taurus, Cancer, Capricorn

The Taurus knows and appreciates the importance of home much as the Virgo does. These two signs can bond over the comfort of the familiar. Your Virgo will appreciate another homebody who doesn't mind spending a lazy weekend at home watching television or curling up with a good book. Cancers are an emotional sign who sympathize deeply with others; and Virgos will bring emotional stability to these feeling animals. The Cancer will flourish with such a sweet and uniquely balanced friend nearby to offer support and quiet encouragement. Capricorns and Virgos are hardworking and motivated and tend to have a magnetic connection to one another.

The Capricorn is capable of bringing a normally shy Virgo out of her shell and out into the world.

If you are single or work from home the Virgo is the cat of your dreams. And while the Virgo can adapt to a number of crazy environments she truly shines against a quiet and unassuming backdrop. A small, homey studio apartment with a settled couple would fit these cats just fine; and, with the right amount of sun exposure and places to tuck away for moments of solitude and thought, the Virgo will be immensely happy. Your Virgo will love you quietly and at times seem to keep her distance, but she will always be there, even if you can't see her. As for other animals in the home, you may find that your Virgo doesn't bond right away with these fellow inhabitants, but she can learn to accept them as an integral part of her routine and life. These relationships may be like ships passing in the night, but with the right amount of space between them, animosity will be minimal.

LIBRA
SEPTEMBER 24 TO OCTOBER 23

JUSTICE-SEEKING, FAIR, WARM, EXPRESSIVE

SYMBOL	The Scales
ELEMENT	Air
QUALITY	Cardinal
RULING HOUSE	Seventh
RULING PLANET	Venus
POLARITY	Masculine
LUCKY STONE	Aquamarine
LUCKY NUMBER	6

PERSONALITY

The symbol for the Libra is two scales in balance. This is a personality based on one desire: fairness. All other emotions and attributes are secondary to the Scales' need for balance. A Libra cat is warm and gentle, but fierce when things are out of alignment. If there is a scuffle, or any malign intentions in the home, the Libra cat will be right in the middle, ready to restore peace. As an air sign, the Libra can be extremely light on her feet and fast.

These cats are natural psychologists, ready for you to unload your problems, so they can silently guide you in the right direction. However, it can be difficult for the Libra to say no, so he may get bowled over by others relatively easily. Venus rules these cats, making them the romantics of the zodiac. The Libra is a flirty cat, chatting

up the other neighborhood cats any chance they get. Their smooth-talking and gentle features make them easy company to keep.

The Scales are energized by the need to balance the world, but they can also be prone to lounging around when things are going right. This isn't necessarily a physical laziness, as the Libra enjoys interacting with the world around him; it's more of an emotional burnout that comes from always acting as referee. Though these cats are multitalented, Libras often need help making a decision. This is the cat who will meow at the door to be let outside only to return a few minutes later to be let back in. These cats need guidance to keep them emotionally steady, but once he is there, it's hard to get a Libra off the right track. These are warm, loving animals with lots of good to spread around.

LIFESTYLE

The Libra loves luxury and he loves to be smothered in attention. Anything that pays tribute to the Libra's physical beauty will be welcomed by these handsome animals. Hair brushes and stylish collars will bring out his true colors. The Libra also makes friends with everyone he meets, so introduce him around the neighborhood. Indigo blue is said to soothe these cats, and the scent of rose will also help your Libra be more decisive. Friday is the Libra's favorite day, so be sure to give one or two extra treats on Fridays to give him the confidence and energy boost he needs to get through the rest of the week without burning out.

The Scales feline is also very creative and needs to be stimulated with puzzles and hard-to-solve games. As a

Cardinal sign, the Libra is a born initiator and is very good at letting his needs be known. Feeding this cat on a schedule is advisable, as the Libra likes dependability in others. Make sure you pay special attention to the Libra's eyes and fur, as these are the most important features to him.

The Cardinal signs have difficulty staying on task because they often go off on their own endeavors and forget the rest of us. To combat this, don't allow your Libra (if he is an outdoor cat) outside whenever he pleases. Keep outdoor time scheduled, so he knows when he'll be going out and when it's time to go back in—you will both keep your sanity instead of constantly waiting for the Scales cat to make up his mind. Trying new treats and new toys with this cat is always a plus. It will keep his mind fresh and his heart eager to keep up diplomatic relations. Without the right amount of stimulus, the Libra can become detached and distant. The evening hours are the best time to spend with him, when he is most at peace and is happy to enjoy his balanced home.

RELATIONSHIPS

BEST MATCHES   Aquarius, Gemini, Sagittarius

The Libra and the Aquarius are the chattier of the zodiac signs and will have lots to discuss with one another. The human Aquarius can spend an entire weekend indoors catching up with the Libra cat. These two signs are also great at supporting each other emotionally. If the Libra cat is down, the Aquarius is bound to pick him up and tell him he is worthy of anything he attempts. The Gemini likes to woo a crowd as much as the Libra, and this is nearly a perfect match. Both are big flirts without feeling the jealousy or competition that may accompany that feature. They both appreciate justice, fairness, and equality in the world. The Sagittarius will never grow bored with a Libra. Fierce and determined, the Sagittarius will push the Libra to dig a bit deeper into himself and to become more fully rounded.

The perfect human-cat pairing for the Scales is someone who can provide a luxurious, balanced environment for this flirtatious and fun animal. Libras get a bad rap for being indecisive, but the truth is that the Libra just wants to squeeze life dry—and there's nothing wrong with that. The Libra wants a partner who will embrace this trait and show Libra his world to make him feel a part of something bigger and more important. The right person will stimulate the Libra's mind and respect his need to be the peacekeeper in any environment. These cats typically get along well with one or two other cats in the home where they can settle disputes, playing the beta and the alpha as the situation requires. The Libra's ability to make friends quickly will help integrate him into a home with roommates, partners, or other animals. Just be sure to get in ample one-on-one time that reassures the Libra you will always be there for him.

SCORPIO

OCTOBER 24 TO NOVEMBER 22

FREE-SPIRITED, BRAVE, FOCUSED,
OPEN-MINDED

SYMBOL	The Scorpion
ELEMENT	Water
QUALITY	Fixed
RULING HOUSE	Eighth
RULING PLANET	Mars
POLARITY	Feminine
LUCKY STONE	Black Opal
LUCKY NUMBER	36

PERSONALITY

The Scorpio is perhaps the bravest of the zodiac signs—so brave, in fact, that there is no worse fate for a Scorpio than a life of predictability. Bold and daring, these cats are not for the faint of heart. If you've come home to your cat balancing on the open freezer door, chances are you own a Scorpio kitty. And the Scorpion is the perfect mascot for these furry acrobats who embody the bravery, toughness, and survivalist traits of the ruthless arachnid. The source of their ambition is often a mystery, which is how the Scorpio prefers things. It's less complicated to have to account for your crazy, wild stunts if you just keep them to yourself. These are the cats that people hook up spy cams for in their house to see what they're up to all day.

The Scorpio is often sold as a jealous, overly ambitious personality, showing little concern for others, but this could not be further from the truth with Scorpio cats. These traits are naturally bred in most cats, but the Scorpio cat has learned how to tone all of these negatives down and to accentuate the positive by letting her human in on some of her trade secrets. The Scorpio is also extremely intuitive and can sense when the mood has shifted in the room before anyone has the chance to say anything.

While she is not so much invested in fixing the problems of others, her bravery can be inspirational to those suffering from a lack of spontaneity or those stuck in a rut. The Scorpion is calculating but doesn't wait too long to before she strikes, which makes her an excellent hunter. The laws of gravity don't apply to these felines, so the best parts of their personality seem to just float out there in the open. It can be beautiful to watch a Scorpio dance in the air for a bug or a bird, or simply run laps around the living room because she can. This kinetic energy will bring happiness to anyone willing to watch her in action.

LIFESTYLE

The Scorpio doesn't like to compete for attention, so she may operate best as an only cat. These are sturdy animals who don't require much in terms of luxuries; but don't plan on a weekend getaway before ensuring that you have a trusted cat sitter in place as the Scorpio prefers not to go long without some attention. Let anyone watching your Scorpion know that she needs positive reinforcement and encouragement to stay on task with good behavior.

The water signs tend to be drawn to the evening hours. Your Scorpio will most likely be active from sunrise to sunset but the evening hours of the day will have her honing her playful skill set. Try some hunting games with her, or take her outside to show her the stars. Fish and light meats are what these cats prefer, and they often prefer it fresh. The

Scorpio will know if you've skimped on the portion or quality of her food, so don't even try it. She'll love to crawl into bed with you in the morning to try and distract you from getting on with the business of your day. This is because she loves you and because she wants you to stay around all day with her so she can show off her newest tricks.

These cats are ruled by the head, so she will want a special place to rub her scents into. A scratching post or a small cat tree, nothing too fancy, will do the trick. These are great animals to travel with and they move around with relative ease. Just be sure she knows home base is with you, and you will have one happy, balanced cat on your hands.

RELATIONSHIPS

BEST MATCHES   Cancer, Capricorn, Pisces

Scorpio is most certainly an alpha and prefers not to have to take a backseat to anyone, especially her human companion. This works well with Cancers, who are typically soft-spoken and like the guidance and boldness that Scorpio displays. Cancers like to feel secure and a Scorpio can provide this. If you've just made a big move to a new city or started a new job, you may find that a new Scorpio friend will help ease the transition for you. Cancers are natural pleasers, which will be music to a Scorpio's ears. They will mew with delight when the Scorpion performs an amazing feat, and encourage activity when the Scorpion gets a bit lazy. The Pisces, another water sign, also tends to be dreamy, but these two signs can be very different, creating a rich chemistry and stimulating relationship.

A human companion for a Scorpio will be a free spirit who encourages growth and, when appropriate, discipline for these brave and well-intentioned cats. The right person will know not to steal too much of the spotlight and that these cats do best when allowed to just be themselves. Whether you're home a lot or like to travel, this is the right cat for you. Scorpios prefer the company of mature companions over developing companions because it allows them to be the only clown and entertainer in the room.

You'll know you're ready for a strong personality like the Scorpion when you find your routine has gotten a bit tedious, or when you can commit to learning how to hold back so someone else can take center stage. The Scorpio's relationships may include distant or cold points, but don't be discouraged: All Scorpios need time to themselves and once they have it, they realize they prefer an audience and the comfort of having others around. Despite their brazenness, these are some of the sweetest, most catlike cats of the zodiac.

SAGITTARIUS

NOVEMBER 23 TO DECEMBER 21

QUICK-WITTED, CHARMING, FUNNY, PHILOSOPHICAL

SYMBOL	The Archer
ELEMENT	Fire
QUALITY	Mutable
RULING HOUSE	Ninth
RULING PLANET	Jupiter
POLARITY	Masculine
LUCKY STONE	Garnet
LUCKY NUMBER	21

PERSONALITY

If you have ever had the pleasure of watching a Sagittarius cat hunt (whether live prey or a toy), you know their deadly accuracy and lightning reflexes make them an alpha predator of the highest caliber. Like his Archer talisman, the Sagittarius cat shoots for the moon and rarely thinks about the consequences should he fall short. These resourceful kitties often transpose these skills into all areas of their lives and flourish in an environment filled with order and meaning. Your Sagittarius is always on the hunt for puzzles he can solve. You may find yourself hiding the treats a little more resourcefully around these cats, as their brains are tapped into a higher level of awareness.

It should come as no surprise to you that the Sagittarius Sun sign is often depicted as a centaur: half man, half horse.

Your cat might display many of the centaur's abilities; smart and agile, these cats prefer high perches and open spaces to hunt or to explore new territory. These cats seem to possess the best of both worlds. They are both athletic and brilliant, and require a lot of mental stimulation to keep their brains fresh and sharp.

The Sagittarius can often be found deep in thought, looking out the window. These are quiet cats who prefer to think things through, but when they do communicate, it can often lead to hilarity. The Sagittarian is a divine humorist with a keen sense of comedic timing. You may come home to find your Sagittarian has discovered how to open doors or balance himself on the living room lamp. Because of his love of order and meaning, your Sagittarian will be especially hard on himself if something goes wrong. Always remember to encourage the adventurous spirit in your cat with lots of praise and new challenges. Also remember that, while Sagittarian cats are highly intelligent, they will make mistakes; so do positively reinforce good behavior.

LIFESTYLE

Your Sagittarius will not want for much. These cats are quiet self-starters who revel in both solitary activities and group fun. Because the Sagittarian kitty loves the hunt, you may want to invest in a food bowl or treat dispenser that makes eating a game. Your cat will also like dark spaces where he can do his best thinking. A kitty tent or a quiet, covered space will allow your Sagittarian to unwind, escape, and plot his next adventure.

These cats make great teachers, and will love to have you follow them around as they show you their world. There isn't much that can rile them up, but they may feel too restless at night, so be sure to leave out lots of games and activities as you sleep so you can get the rest you need, and your cat can have his essential sensory experiences at his paw tips. The Sagittarian, if he is an indoor kitty, will need new smells and sounds every day; otherwise he might be tempted into negative behaviors that will leave both you and him unsatisfied. If you can, leave a window open during the day so your cat can interact with the world around him. Or you may want to purchase a harness to take the Sagittarius out for nature walks. It can be a challenge to keep these cats from getting bored, but there are plenty of opportunities to turn your living space into the creative home environment they require.

Be aware that these active cats require a healthy diet that supports the joints, particularly the hips, as they enjoy leaping and high acrobatics. This is why string toys and lasers will be your Sagittarian's best friends. Making life comfortable for a Sagittarius shouldn't be a challenge—that is the beauty of owning one of these low-maintenance felines—but don't forget to give these cats the adventurous life they deserve!

RELATIONSHIPS

That Sagittarian cat works well with some of the other outgoing signs, such as the Leo and the Aries. These signs tend to be gregarious leaders, yet they lack the emotional maturity of the Sagittarius. The Sagittarius will guide with his quiet yet brave nature. You may find yourself implementing some of your cat's behaviors at work or in your own relationships. Learn to branch out and take calculated chances just like your Sagittarius. These cats will love to make you laugh with their high jinks. A Sagittarius cat will work best with someone who appreciates his comedic genius (even when he knocks over a few houseplants to get you to laugh)!

Sagittarius is ruled by a big planet, Jupiter, which means you can expect to have a larger-than-life companion in your Sagittarian cat. The daring Sagittarius will love being paired with someone who is gregarious and nurtures an explorative nature. Your cat may not always want to be the boss, but when he does, he knows what he's doing, so be sure to follow his lead. The Sagittarius, while adventurous, is rarely spontaneous without regard for his surroundings. He is intuitive and will read your emotions carefully. The Sagittarius is not known as the cuddliest in the zodiac, but he can, and will, show affection in his own way. Look out for your cat signaling he wants to be close to you. He may wait for you at the door after work with a toy, or he may wind in and out of your legs while you make dinner. Be sure to reward these shows of affection with some intentional playtime and you will be rewarded in return with more affection. These cats require at least fifteen minutes a day of high-energy games and chase. Your friend will love to be up with you early in the morning, so it may be best to play before work and before bedtime to stem any nocturnal races across your bed. The Sagittarius may test your patience from time to time; this means you need to freshen up your routine. Play some bird sounds or buy a fresh catnip plant and watch your Sagittarius's behavior flourish.

CAPRICORN

DECEMBER 22 TO JANUARY 20

PUNCTUAL, RESOURCEFUL, DEDICATED, REGAL

SYMBOL	The Goat
ELEMENT	Earth
QUALITY	Cardinal
RULING HOUSE	Tenth
RULING PLANET	Saturn
POLARITY	Feminine
LUCKY STONE	Topaz
LUCKY NUMBER	1

PERSONALITY

Like all of the Cardinal signs, the Capricorn is an animal fixated on loyalty and predictability. What makes these creatures special is their ability to be both selfless and self-motivated. Your Capricorn kitty will enjoy waking up in the morning with a schedule to look forward to, and preferably you will follow that schedule to a T. These are cats who don't require you to dote on them, but they will likely dote on you. Capricorn cats are selfless with their energy and time and will always take a warm lap over a fancy cat tower. These cats maintain their temperament and it's hard to move them to either end of the emotional spectrum.

Those who don't know Capricorns well might be inclined to believe these cats are dull, but it is quite the opposite: The Capricorn's predictability makes her an excellent comfort companion. Capricorns are not easily swayed by the emotions of others, and they are great listeners. They flourish in chaotic environments and can provide some much needed balance to a home inhabited by creatures born under different signs. A Capricorn can also be saucy when the situation is right. A husky meow or delicate tap of the paw on your arm is her way of telling you she is ready for your undivided attention.

Capricorns' loyalty makes them attractive pets; and, once they open up to you, they can be extremely personable and vocal. These cats make excellent additions to homes with lots of action, and they will walk from room to room soaking it all up and adding their own input when they feel it is necessary. Your Capricorn will be happiest when she is on a feeding, petting, and playing schedule. Her personality will make her wise beyond her years. Capricorn kittens may not be prone to as many kittenish antics as many of the other signs: climbing curtains, chasing tails, or swatting at shoelaces may not intrigue her as much as watching you open and shut doors or discovering new parts of her environment. She is a great puzzle solver with a knack for knowing exactly when you need a warm and understanding ear.

LIFESTYLE

The Capricorn cat is prepared to weather all seasons, so she won't require anything too fancy. Her tacit and reserved nature will make it easy for her to find a warm chair or a laptop left open on which to make herself at home. If you do choose to purchase something elaborate for your Capricorn like a window seat, gourmet dinner, or an expensive scratching post, she will most likely ignore the intended gift and prefer to nestle up in the box it came in.

The Capricorn is known to outlast many of the other signs in the zodiac, most likely due to her mellow nature, so don't be surprised if your Capricorn lives many healthy years. A large part of a Capricorn's health is her teeth. Be sure her diet supports good dental health, as this is a practical measure to ensure longevity, and she will repay you

with lots of lap time and purring. Capricorns are known for their love of fish, so a few fish treats here and there will give her a healthy snack and an occasional welcome break from routine. You'll probably find that if you sleep past the time your Capricorn eats, she will gently remind you with a paw to the nose or a decent meow in your sleeping ear to help remind you.

These cats do great with human and cat roommates alike, and will flourish with an open-door policy that allows them to choose their favorite spots to nap in throughout the day. But since your Capricorn is loyal, you will most likely find her at the foot of your bed each night. The Capricorn is one of the easiest cats to keep company with: Feed her on time, offer her lots of space and love when requested, and reap the benefits of befriending these mellow, loyal, and wonderful felines.

RELATIONSHIPS

BEST MATCHES   Taurus, Pisces, Virgo

Capricorns are motivated and predictable, so they form the strongest relationships with humans and other cats who give them a bit of the opposite. For this reason, Pisces and Virgos will do well under the reasonable Capricorn's influence. The Pisces and Virgo felines are free-spirited and feisty and will grow with some guidance from the Capricorn. The Taurus is another Earth-centered sign that can be cool under pressure like the Capricorn. These two signs complement each other well, and often find themselves sitting peacefully next to each other, soaking up the warm vibes.

Your cat will love a fun and flexible relationship with the people around her, especially you. Don't be afraid to show your real colors around your Capricorn; she is not out to judge you. Let her know when your day is rough and she'll most likely close her eyes and soothingly purr. You'll start to feel your blood pressure lower and your pulse begin to even out.

Give your Capricorn reason to trust you by following her cues. If she likes to be brushed, do it routinely and throw out some well-deserved compliments about her healthy coat. Just as you find her purrs relaxing, she will love to hear you speak in soft, even tones. Capricorns are great cats to integrate into a house with roommates because it gives them a chance to work up the social ladder, and the Capricorn is always looking for ways to improve herself. Don't be offended if you find your kitty lounging on your roommate's bed, or if you find her chatting up your friends at the dinner table; she is merely expanding her interpersonal horizons. Loyalty is the strongest facet of the Capricorn cat, and you can depend on her to sense when you need her most. If there are other cats in your home, your Capricorn will assess her position in the pack immediately, and she will most certainly work her way to the top quickly. It's very hard to anger a Capricorn. With the Capricorn's propensity for good health, you can expect a relationship full of mutual respect, love, and dedication for many, many years.

AQUARIUS

JANUARY 21 TO FEBRUARY 18

CARING, HILARIOUS, IDEALISTIC, ENGAGING

SYMBOL	The Water Carrier
ELEMENT	Air
QUALITY	Fixed
RULING HOUSE	Eleventh
RULING PLANET	Saturn
POLARITY	Masculine
LUCKY STONE	Turquois
LUCKY NUMBER	17

PERSONALITY

Aquarians are the great humanitarians (or "catitar-ians") of the zodiac. They care about all beings in their realm and embody the image of the water carrier perfectly. They relish taking on the burdens of others in spite of the personal consequences they may face. These cats are great thinkers and teachers with soft souls and big spirits. They love to make others laugh, to make them feel well and whole. They can be extremely idealistic and dreamy, but only because they want the best for the world. These are the cats you see on the news caring for abandoned baby chicks or other helpless creatures. If you have a physical wound, your Aquarian will want to heal you by licking you or lying on it. While it may not physically feel great, the emotional benefits these cats offer are terrific.

Like a few other signs in the zodiac, they can be difficult to keep on task, but they are easy to redirect because they put a lot of their faith in others to guide them. Your Aquarian is a lovable goof with a big heart who may forget to eat breakfast or to wipe his paws clean when he steps outside of the litter box, but he lives a big and beautiful life. Don't let the goofiness fool you, either. You will see the Aquarian staring off into space frequently. This is because he is busy having big thoughts about the world around him and he is much more in tune with the world than people give him credit for. He carries a lot on his shoulders without ever letting on. These cats want to simplify life, not complicate it, so they may have trouble adjusting to new cats, people, or situations. However, with a bit of prodding they will come to see that change is a good thing, as would any philosopher worth his salt. The Aquarian is capable of great loneliness without purpose and can feel the hurt of others too deeply. Reassure your water carrier that he doesn't always have to be the comforter and that it's OK to be the one receiving the comforting.

LIFESTYLE

The Aquarian lives a no-frills lifestyle, and you may find yourself accidentally underserving him breakfast or dinner. Because the Aquarius isn't one to step on toes when something goes wrong, you may actually have to force yourself and him to indulge once in a while. Sit in his favorite spot and invite him into your lap for some belly rubs and scratches. Leave a few windows cracked so he has some nice sensory input to go along with his big thinking. He will likely hang out in wide open spaces and will like to follow in your footsteps.

Sleeping with an Aquarius is a treat because Aquarians are both cuddly and considerate of the needs of others—which means more foot and elbow room for you. The Aquarian may neglect himself from time to time. Make sure you trim his coat if he is a long-haired fellow. And keep an eye on his nails—because he will likely not want to mess up your furniture, but he is still a cat, and may indulge in that bad habit too, if only once in a great while. Almost any negative behavior can be trained out of an Aquarian. These cats enjoy being taught tricks. You may have the best luck bathroom training Aquarians because of their water-carrying background and their smarts.

Keeping the Aquarian indoors shouldn't be a challenge as long as you're home and have a nice, big comfy couch or bed for him to lounge on. Aquarians are great city-dwelling or apartment cats. They tend to live long and healthy lives as long as they feel useful to the people around them. It is believed that Saturn, the ruling planet of Aquarius, was created to teach us something about others and to make us into guides for others. We all have something to learn from these gentle felines.

RELATIONSHIPS

BEST MATCHES   Sagittarius, Libra, Gemini

It's practically impossible to find a bad match for an Aquarian because they are the ultimate givers, but there are a few signs that work particularly well with these cats. The Sagittarius has the same sunny disposition as the Aquarian and the same hopefulness. Like the Aquarian, the Sagittarian can also get off track, so these two signs tend to get a little dreamy when paired together, but they are also a genuine and sweet pairing who are built to be life-long friends. Like the Aquarian, Libra is a "people cat" and enjoys floating from room to room meeting new people. Unlike the Aquarian, the Libra enjoys making new friends to gain more knowledge about the creatures around him.

This will help the Aquarius break out of his routine and it will help him build his social skills. The Gemini rarely makes waves and, just like the Aquarian, doesn't typically harbor ill will. These two will bask in the glow of meeting another creature who just gets it.

With so many happy traits, it's hard to see why a person would turn down the chance to love and care for an Aquarius; these cats do best with human companions who live life at full throttle and need to unburden themselves from time to time. This is where the Aquarius will find his purpose and his reason for being. Other cats will love the calming, wise-natured Aquarius and will be drawn to his knowledge and sweetness. Roommates and friends may try to walk out with your cat tucked under an arm when they see how sweet and sensitive he's capable of being. Perhaps the hardest part of being with an Aquarian is sharing him with all of the admirers he is bound to collect in his time on Earth. With these philanthropic cats you will find a friend who listens, talks only when necessary, and comforts always—a loving, lifelong companion.

PISCES

FEBRUARY 19 TO MARCH 20

CARING, ADAPTIVE, ENTHUSED, INSPIRED

SYMBOL	The Fish
ELEMENT	Water
QUALITY	Mutable
RULING HOUSE	Twelfth
RULING PLANET	Neptune
POLARITY	Feminine
LUCKY STONE	Amethyst
LUCKY NUMBER	7

PERSONALITY

Perhaps the most creative sign of them all, the Fish cat knows what it's like living in two worlds. The Pisces cat may seem like a contradiction of traits, but this cat is versatile and adaptive to almost any situation you can throw at her. Throwing a wild house party over the weekend? The Pisces cat will throw herself at the feet of your guests. She is loved by all, but understood by few. This is perhaps her best charm: mystery. Some days she will be the most gregarious cat you have ever met, with her many vocalizations and attempts at self-petting, and the next day she will be elusive and hard to find. This is because the Pisces struggles to choose which world to live in from one day to the next. This, one might think, would lead to tension and unhappiness; but the Fish is

able to swim through all types of water without feeling trapped. The Pisces cat will do the same.

Don't mistake the quiet version of your Pisces for aloofness. She is simply trying to figure out how to navigate the complex nature of being a wild animal in a civilized world. There is no way to tame a Pisces' behavior, it comes and it goes like tides, but she prefers this flux as it feels most natural in her world. Without the ability to choose her own schedule during the day, the Pisces can become overwhelmed easily. She will excel in an environment where she's allowed to use her imagination to shape the day. With routine comes laziness for the Pisces, and while it's not uncommon for older cats to nap for many hours of the day, your Pisces may be napping out of boredom. Don't forget to honor her wild and free personality by letting her be whatever she wants to be, day to day.

LIFESTYLE

The Fish cat is incredibly adept at blending into her environment. She makes everything look like a downstream swim, but don't mistake this laid-back behavior as a lack of desire for human interaction—these cats love people. Having a lot of different personalities to interact with is an integral part of the Pisces' mental health regimen. Invite friends over and take turns playing with this fun kitty. These are dreamy felines who will notice light changes and the smallest bug in the corner of the room, because they are astute observers and creative thinkers. You may want to purchase a laser pointer or hang crystals in the living room to create rainbows of light for your cat to go nuts over. However, don't forget to reward her efforts with a treat or a fuzzy mouse toy to catch after all her hard work.

Pisces cats love all things soft and fluffy, so be prepared to give up a pillow or two to these cats. If your Pisces is an outdoor cat, you will probably find she likes to explore. She may make a lot of friends with your neighbors and the other animals outside. Because she is a dreamy cat, she may wander off from time to time in search of a bird or a butterfly and you may need to draw her back home with a can of tuna or something equally delicious. If your Pisces is an indoor cat, she will likely stake out her claim somewhere cool and dark, a place that echoes the feel of her water roots. When you leave for work, leave the bedroom light off and the door ajar to give her a calming spot to lounge in while you're out.

The Pisces needs to feel close to her human companion when the mood strikes her, so she may end up sleeping at the head of your bed or, when she's feeling really friendly, on your chest. It's probably not surprising that the Pisces loves food from the sea; after all she is both a cat and a water sign. A little tuna and a little imaginative play is all it takes to keep these funny cats happy.

RELATIONSHIPS

BEST MATCHES   Scorpio, Cancer, Capricorn

Imaginative minds that tend wander in far-off places during the day and enjoy engaging new and exciting people and experiences will jive perfectly with the Pisces. The perfect Pisces companion is easy to please, but also has a strong, centered sense of self. The creative type looking for some divine inspiration will love the whimsical and dreamy Pisces cat.

Scorpios and Pisces bond almost instantaneously, fueled by a mutual desire to experience the world in nontraditional ways. The Pisces looks to the Scorpion's sensibilities for protection and affection. In the Cancer, the Pisces finds mutual passion and understanding. The Cancer is much

more of a doer than the Pisces, but both are capable of great creativity and can be good artistic companions. Although the Capricorn is the polar opposite of the Pisces, this union is filled with balance and harmony and can both ground and inspire both parties.

You will probably find that your Pisces is more curious than invested in relationships with other animals. She may be amused by dogs or other cats but won't necessarily become best friends with the neighbor's feline. If you're living in a multi-cat home, your Pisces will probably build meaningful relationships with her cat brethren, but she'll need to trust them first. Give her time to adjust if you are bringing her or another cat into the home; giving her the power to greet these new friends on her own terms will have the best results.

ACKNOWLEDGMENTS

I want to thank all of the good people in the world who choose to rescue and spend their lives with cats. I want to thank my own cats, Bill Murray, Grover, and Liz Lemon, who bring infinite joy to my life. I would like to thank my family, friends, and my wife, Aileen, for supporting my feline obsessions. I would like to thank beautiful soul, fellow cat lover, and incredible editor, Courtney Drew, for the opportunity to bring this wonderful idea to fruition. Thank you to Vikki Chu for the smashing artwork, to Hillary Caudle for such a delightful design, and to the whole Chronicle crew for running such a smooth and fun operation, and for allowing me to be part of such a fantastic project.